© Scripture Union 2019
ISBN 978 1 78506 748 8

Scripture Union England and Wales
Trinity House, Opal Court, Opal Drive, Fox Milne,
Milton Keynes, MK15 0DF
email: info@scriptureunion.org.uk
www.scriptureunion.org.uk

The right of Lucy Pearson to be identified as the author of
this work has been asserted by her in accordance with the
Copyright, Designs and Patents Act 1988.

British Library Cataloguing-in-Publication Data
A catalogue record of this book is available from the
British Library.

Printed and bound in Malta by Melita Press

Cover and internal design: Gemma Willis

Scripture Union is an international Christian charity
working with churches in more than 130 countries.

Thank you for purchasing this book. Any profits from this book
support SU in England and Wales to bring the good news of
Jesus Christ to children, young people and families and to
enable them to meet God through the Bible and prayer.

Find out more about our work and how you can get involved at:
www.scriptureunion.org.uk (England and Wales)
www.suscotland.org.uk (Scotland)
www.suni.co.uk (Northern Ireland)
www.scriptureunion.org (USA)
www.su.org.au (Australia)

'I HAVE LOVED BEING ABLE TO TALK WITH SOMEONE ABOUT WHO I AM AND FOR SOMEONE TO LISTEN FOR ONCE'

– Rachel, 13

Rooted is not a programme, it's not something that you 'do' for ten weeks with a group of young people.

Rooted is a way of being, a way of thinking about long-term relational ministry with young people. Rooted works in any context, with any level of faith development and with any level of ability.

Rooted is adaptable, accessible, invitational and creative.

The Rooted model places the young person at the centre, and seeks to provide space for that young person to grow, flourish and be nurtured in a safe, committed and compassionate Christian community.

Rooted aims to unlock the potential in each young person, enabling them to be the very best version of themselves, enabling them to be all that God intended them to be.

Rooted embraces the messiness of life and encourages young people to wrestle with big questions authentically.

The material contained within this resource gives you ideas for helping young people to explore their identity and self-worth.

As a leader, you have the privilege to journey alongside these young people and help them in their exploration, whilst sharing something of your own journey so far. You will notice that there is very little in the way of explicit 'faith discussion' or 'God-slot'-type material. Instead, within the material for each theme, you will find several prompts and questions for leaders designed to open up discussion around sharing testimonies or exploring the Bible. I hope that you will naturally, authentically and appropriately share your own experience of how faith and life meld together as you spend time with your group.

Rooted isn't about the activities you 'do', the venue you 'inhabit' or the resources you can provide. It is about facilitating genuine conversation that develops positive, meaningful and long-term relationships.

The Rooted material in this resource covers nine key themes (outlined on the next page) and is designed to be adaptable to any context. The suggestions for activities are exactly that – suggestions. You should absolutely expect to mould and shape them to suit your context and the young people you are working with. The tenth session will help you explore 'What next?' for your group.

If you're not already in contact with a group of young people, you might be wondering how you can even begin to develop Rooted in your community. At the end of this book you'll find some advice on running your own Rooted Hub - a tried and tested approach that will help you make initial connections with young people in your area.

I pray that God will use you to share his love with young people as they discover what difference his love can make to the challenges and adventures of life.

Lucy Pearson
Scripture Union, Greater Manchester Development Worker
Rooted Pioneer

THE SEED - WHO AM I?

THE SOIL - WHERE AM I?

NEW GROWTH - WHO WILL I BE?

EXTRA BITS AND PIECES

WHERE DO I BEGIN?

A few questions to consider before embarking
on the Rooted journey...

- Who are you working with? Why are you doing this?
*(For advice on making initial connections with young people in your
community turn to the 'Rooted Hubs' section at the back of this book)*

- Who will work with you on your Rooted team?

- Where will you meet?

- What resources do you have?

- What are the young people expecting?

- How will you explain to the young people what Rooted is?

- Are these young people exploring faith?

- Are there any particular issues that you want to focus on?

- How might you look to adapt some of the material in this
resource to better suit your context? *(eg If the group you are
working with doesn't enjoy creativity - what activity would they enjoy?
Perhaps sport, drama, outdoor activities, etc. How can you make sure
your activities will help you to relay the message?)*

- Have you made sure that your group gatherings will
adhere to the safeguarding policies of your organisation?
What additional pastoral support will you offer? *(You might
consider a mentoring programme and/or referrals to other agencies
or key workers.)*

- What's next? (See page 44 for a few ideas.)

WHAT IS MY NAME?

Objectives:

- For the group to get to know one another and gain an understanding of what their time together will be about.

- For the leaders to gain an understanding of the group dynamic.

EXPLORING IDENTITY

This may be the first time the group has met and some may be feeling uneasy. It's good to take the opportunity to make it clear that this is a safe space for them to explore new ideas, ask big questions and try new skills – but most importantly, it is a space for them to be themselves.

Identity can be a challenging subject for many young people, so be prepared for some difficult, but honest conversations. Make sure you have created a structure, in line with your organisation's safeguarding policy, around your Rooted group that offers extra support to young people who need it. This might include a mentoring programme, referrals to other agencies or key workers.

Suggested activities

Discussion
My name

Invite each person in the group to share the meaning of their name – if they know it! (If they don't know, a quick google should help!) Talk about the importance of names – and how they form a foundational part of identity. If someone asks who you are, usually the first response is to say your name.

After this, hand out copies of the 'All about me' worksheet (available to photocopy from page 59) and invite each young person to take a few minutes to fill it in. Make it clear that you will keep hold of their completed sheets until the end of the course when they'll be asked to complete a similar task exploring their Rooted journey.

Game
Would You rather

Talk briefly about the importance of the decisions and choices we make in forming our identity. Then play a simple game of 'Would you rather?' – giving young people a simple choice between two conflicting scenarios (listed below). Encourage the young people to move to one end of your meeting space if they would choose one option, and to the other end for the other option.

Would you rather:

- *eat mayonnaise on ice cream, or eat ice cream with mushy peas?*

- *always smell of onions or always burp loudly before speaking?*

- *be sad forever, but live in a beautiful mansion, or live in a shed and be happy?*

- *have a dog that loves you but poos in your room, or have a cat that hates you but never makes a mess?*

- *watch as much TV as you like, but only on CBBC, or only watch 15 minutes a week of whatever you want?*

- *be forced to listen to hard core rock constantly, or never listen to any music again?*

- *eat garlic bread for breakfast every day, or eat a jar of jam for dinner every day?*

- *wear a superhero outfit to school or be forced to wear your school clothes every weekend?*

After the game, remind the young people that today you will be inviting them to explore what really makes them who they are.

Reflection
Exploring identity
(pieces of card, pens)

Explain to the young people that the way we feel and think about ourselves is an important part of who we are. Give out pieces of card and pens, then invite the group to write down any words that come to mind when they hear the word 'identity'. Share the responses.

Community
Valuing respect
(paper, pens)

It's important that everyone in the group respects one another – including leaders. Explain to everyone that the time spent in this group is valuable and therefore it is a time where everyone must respect one another, respect leaders and respect the venue.

Hand out paper and pens and invite each group member to write down three 'rules' they think would help to grow a positive sense of community as you work together.

Bring all the ideas together and establish eight 'rules' that everyone can agree on. Display these in your meeting space whenever you meet.

Creative space
Collage
(magazines, photos, glue, scissors, coloured paper, pens, pencils, assorted craft materials)

Spread a variety of craft materials around the room. Explain to the young people that they now have an opportunity to express who they are, using the materials provided.

This is a good opportunity for leaders to get to know their group as conversations evolve whilst the young people create.

Faith exploration
God values everyone

During the collage activity (or another activity of your choosing) you could use the following questions to open up conversations with young people individually, or in small groups.

- *Have you ever wondered if God is really there?*
- *Have you ever thought about who God says you are?*
- *Do you believe your life has a purpose?*
- *What would it feel like if you knew that you were created to be you and only you by the one who created the world?*

You might choose to have some Bible verses printed out on small pieces of paper and spread them around the room whilst the young people engage in the collage activity. Encourage them to read the verses and add them to their collages, if they wish. Talking through with each young person what a particular Bible verse means to you, and why, will help to open up a faith exploration conversation.

You could also ask a leader to speak about how they believe God values and loves everyone – either as the young people engage in an activity, or simply as they sit and listen.

WHAT'S MY JOURNEY?

Objective:

- For young people to understand that their journey matters and that the everyday is just as important as the big things in life.

- For young people to understand that they are valuable.

SHARING STORIES

In the 'What's my name?' session, the young people explored their identity through the lens of what they like, and they reflected on the importance of their own names. In this session they will have the opportunity to explore their life story – their journey so far – and how this has shaped their identity. As you prepare, consider your own journey and how much of your story you are comfortable sharing.

Suggested activities

Introduction
Revisit the previous session

Remind the young people of the theme from the last session and invite them to respond to the following questions:

Has anything happened since we last met that made you think about our last session together?

If so, what was it, and what did it make you think about?

Reflection
Dreaming big

Ask the young people the following question and encourage them to share their responses:

If you could live anywhere, where would it be?

Discussion
Celebrity Stories

Prior to your time together, find and print out pictures of current famous people or influencers when they were younger. Research their stories and make a few notes. Stick the pictures on the walls of your venue, or perhaps have them on a tablet/screen that young people can see.

Ask the young people if they can identify the famous people or influencers in the pictures.

Then pick a few of the famous people or influencers and share their stories – noting where they are from and what they have achieved...

Depending on your group, you might also choose to share the stories of some key biblical characters, such Mary, Esther or Ruth. You might also choose to share some of your own story here too.

Invite the group to reflect on the following questions and share their responses:

What is your biggest achievement* – large or small?
What did it feel like?

Depending on how well your group know one another, they may prefer to draw or write their responses to these questions – and only a few may be willing to share.

* Be aware that for some young people this question may be difficult, as they may not feel they have achieved much at all. Try to help them explore their everyday achievements, such as coming to your session today, or choosing to be generous instead of selfish, etc.

Creative space
Your day

Lay out a roll of lining paper across your meeting space. Ask the young people to imagine that the start of the paper is the start of their day (today) and the end of the paper is right now. Invite them to write or draw everything that has happened in their day so far, thinking in detail.
Once everyone has drawn out their day, ask them to stand back and look at the roll of paper. Ask them to take a moment to reflect on the following two questions:

What or who influenced you?
What or who did you influence?

Remind the young people that every detail of their day is an important part of their life journey.

Reflection
Your Journey

Hand out sheets of paper and pens and encourage each young person to draw a timeline that represents their life. It should start with the day they were born and continue to the

present day, marking out key events, people and places, etc. If the young people are not sure what to include, you could ask some questions to help them reflect:

- *Which teacher has influenced you most?*
- *Who were you best friends with in Year 6?*
- *Have you ever moved house?*
- *Have you been on any significant holidays?*
- *Do you have a favourite film? When did you first see it?*
- *Do you have a favourite song? When did you first hear it?*
- *Have you been on any school trips?*
- *Which members of your family should be added?*
- *What has been your happiest memory?*
- *What has been your saddest memory?*

Allow time for the young people to share their journey sheets, if they would like to. Take the opportunity to share a little of your own journey too. Remember that some young people may never have had this opportunity to reflect on the events that have shaped their lives, and some may need extra time for reflection and discussion.

Faith exploration
God cares about your life

During the reflective activity (or another activity of your choosing) you could use the following questions to open up conversations with young people individually, or in small groups.

- *Do you think God has anything to do with your life?*
- *If you were to thank God for something or someone, what would*

you say?

- *Are there things in your life journey that make you feel angry towards God?*

- *If you could ask God one thing, what would it be?*

As you talk with the young people, make sure you allow them to share their thoughts openly. You may find they raise big questions like 'Why does God let bad stuff happen?' Be honest and real with the young people as these first sessions are setting the foundation for your time together.

You could also ask a leader to speak about the difference God has made in their life – either as the young people engage in an activity, or simply as they sit and listen.

WHAT DO I FEEL?

Objective:

- For young people to have a safe space to explore their emotions and coping mechanisms.

UNDERSTANDING EMOTIONS

In the previous session, the group explored their own journey - reflecting on the people and experiences that have shaped who they are. In this session, young people will have the opportunity to explore their own identity, their own emotions and their own response to the challenges of life.

Suggested activities

Introduction
Revisit the previous session

Remind the young people of the theme from the last session and invite them to respond to the following questions:

Has anything happened since we last met that made you think about our last session together?

If so, what was it, and what did it make you think about?

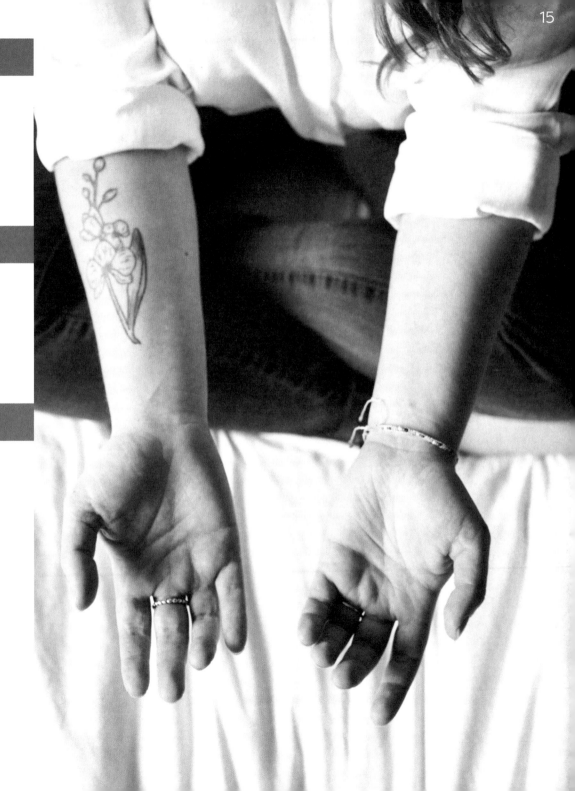

Discussion
Dreaming big

Ask the group the following question:

If you could do the same thing every day, what would it be?

Invite the young people to respond, and then say that each of us enjoys doing different things, we respond in different ways and adapt differently according to our personalities.

Game
Would you rather?

You might have played 'Would you rather?' in a previous session, thinking about different choices. This game is similar but the question is, 'What would you do?'

Designate one part of the room as 'A' and another part as 'B'. Read out the questions below and ask the group to choose which side of the room to go to. Remind the group that this is their own personal choice, so they shouldn't be afraid to be the only person in an area.

1. You walk out of the toilets with toilet roll on your shoe and someone points it out. Do you...

   A) walk off quickly, looking embarrassed? B) laugh it off?

2. You are daydreaming in class and the teacher asks you a question, but you don't know what she said. Do you...

   A) ask them to repeat the question? B) make something up?

3. You realise your friends have left you out of something. Do you...

   A) stop speaking to them? B) confront them and ask why?

4. You see someone upset in the hall. Do you...

   A) ask if they are OK? B) leave it to their mates to sort out, as you don't want to feel nosy?

5. You wake up late and your day starts really badly. You can't wait to get to school to talk about your eventful day, but your friend is really low. Do you...

   A) make them listen to your story first? B) listen to them and forget about yourself?

6. You get to school in a really good mood and your friend is being really mopey and sad. Do you...

   A) try and cheer them up? B) avoid them as you don't want your mood to be affected?

7. You have had a rubbish day. Do you...

   A) do something active to keep your mind off it? B) watch TV/YouTube/Netflix?

8. You work really hard at a test, but get a lower mark than you expected. Do you...

   A) shrug it off and try again next time? B) complain to your teacher?

Think of more questions, if you can, and adapt them to your group.

Reflection
Picturing emotions

Give each member of the group a sheet of paper and access to colouring pens or pencils. Explain that you are going to say four different words, and you would like them to draw what each word makes them think of (a scenario, object, etc).

Encourage the young people to think about the colours they choose to use and why, and to reflect on what each word can actually make them feel physically, eg worry can make you feel sick or have tummy ache.

The words are: jealousy, worry, joy, excitement.

(Leaders should join in with this reflective activity.)

Ask if anyone in the group feels comfortable to share what they have drawn. Don't force anyone, and don't be afraid of silences. It is really valuable to allow the group to hear how other people experience emotion so they can see that everyone is different, and also that they may not be the only one to experience certain things when thinking about emotions.

Creative Space
Jars of joy

(empty pots or jars, paper, coloured pencils, tissue paper, glue sticks, stickers, sticker jewels, felt-tip pens, scissors)

Spend a few minutes talking about how emotions can take over, and sometimes we can respond by engaging in things that aren't helpful when we feel a certain way. Be aware that for some young people this may be a particularly difficult area, so ensure you have appropriate support in place outside of this session. (This may include a mentoring programme or referrals to other agencies or key workers.)

Invite the group to create 'jars of joy'. Explain that the young people can decorate these jars using the materials you've provided, and then they should fill them with slips of paper containing things that they know can help them to feel positive. Ask each young person to write their list of positive things on a sheet of paper and then cut them into strips (with one positive thing on each strip), roll them up and put them into their decorated jar.

You might like to suggest a few examples of positive things, eg being outside, swimming, painting, reading a book, watching Netflix.

Whilst everyone is making their 'jar of joy', explain that when they feel low at home, they can pick out an action from their jar and then do what it says. This can be an important technique for fighting overwhelming negative emotions with positivity, and can help the young people learn what actions may lead to feeling better.

If appropriate for your group, you could print out several positive Bible verses on strips of paper and invite the young people to add them to their jars.

Faith exploration
Knowing God can make a difference to your emotions

During the 'Jars of joy' activity (or another activity of your choosing) you could use the following questions to open up conversations with young people individually, or in small groups.

- *Why do you think God created emotions?*
- *Do you think God experiences emotions?*
- *Have you spoken to God about how you're feeling?*
- *Did you know that we can be honest and real with God, and that he cares about every part of our lives?*

You could also ask a leader to speak about how knowing God impacts their choices and emotions.

HOW DO I SEE MYSELF?

Objective:

- For young people to spend time recognising their strengths, and to support others as they explore their self-worth.

EXPLORING SELF-WORTH

Working together and recognising other people's skills is an important part of life. However, it's easy to spend so much time comparing ourselves to others that we can ignore how incredible we are and who we have been made to be (this is just as true for adults as it is for young people!).

Suggested activities

Introduction
Revisit the previous session

Remind the young people of the theme from the last session and invite them to respond to the following questions:

Has anything happened since we last met that made you think about our last session together?

If so, what was it, and what did it make you think about?

Discussion
Who would you be?

Ask the group the following question:

If you could be anyone in the world, who would you be?

Invite the young people to respond, and share your own response.

Game
Human knot

Invite the group to stand in a circle. They should join hands with one another across the circle (each hand connecting to a different person) creating a 'human knot' as they go. They should then work together to untangle themselves (without loosing hands).

Do this a few times until the group easily succeed and then ask them to try again, but this time they must solve the knot without speaking.

Game
Signs

Invite the group to stand in a circle, and choose one person to stand in the middle. Choose one young person in the circle to be the first 'sign-maker'. This person should come up with a sign (hand or body gesture) that can be passed around the circle without the person in the middle noticing. If the sign is spotted by the person in the middle, they then swap places with the sign-maker. Another sign-maker should then be selected and play continues.

Creative space
SWOT shields

Hand out sheets of paper and pens and invite each person in the group to draw a shield shape and split it into four sections. They should label the sections: **S**trengths, **W**eaknesses, **O**pportunities and **T**hreats.

Encourage the young people to draw or write something about themselves in each section. (You may need to help the group to understand what they should put in the 'threats' section – anything that they feel holds them back or they are fearful of.)

When everyone has finished, discuss the following questions with the group:

How does it feel to see what you are capable of?
Do your strengths outweigh your weaknesses?

Remind the group that knowing what their weaknesses are – what they may need to improve on (like patience or empathy), is actually a strength! Say that no one is perfect, but being aware of who we are can help us step into our full potential, and to support others in doing the same.

Reflection
Letter to a friend

Give each member of the group a sheet of paper with their own name written at the top. Make sure that the top of the paper is folded over so the young people can't see their names – and tell them not to look!

Challenge them to imagine they are writing a letter to a friend with advice relating to everyday life – a letter of support and kindness to build them up.

When they've finished, invite the young people to unfold the top of the paper. They will see that they've written a letter to themselves.

Say that sometimes we can ignore our own advice – even the advice we would choose to give to a friend. Explain that being kind to yourself is an important part of a healthy daily routine and can be helpful in knowing how to support others who are going through a challenging time.

Faith exploration
Knowing God loves you just as you are

During the 'SWOT shields' activity (or another activity of your choosing), you could use the following questions to open up conversations with young people individually, or in small groups.

- *Do you think God is proud of who you are?*
- *Do you think he cares?*
- *Do you know that God sees you and thinks you're incredible?*

You could also ask a leader to share an example of how God uses the least likely people throughout the Bible to do amazing things (eg Bathsheba, Mary, David, etc).

If appropriate, you might choose to ask your group if anyone would like to be prayed for (you may need to explain what prayer is, if the group is unsure!) - or you could have a prayer box or question box available.

WHO'S AROUND ME?

Objective:

- For young people to reflect on their friendships and the choices they make.

FRIENDSHIP AND CHOICES

The previous session gave young people the opportunity to reflect on their skills and qualities, as well as exploring the value of self-care.

In this session, the group will explore what they look for in those they choose to spend time with, and what they bring to their existing relationships.

Prior to this session you will need to create a list of words that describe desirable qualities in a friend (eg truthful, honest, respectful, trustworthy, funny etc). Your list should contain 10 to 12 words. You will need to print/write out a 'pack of words' for each young person, consisting of slips of paper, with one word on each. You will also need an extra 'pack of words' printed/written out at a larger size for the whole group to use together.

Suggested activities

Introduction
Revisit the previous session

Remind the young people of the theme from the last session and invite them to respond to the following questions:

Has anything happened since we last met that made you think about our last session together?

If so, what was it, and what did it make you think about?

Discussion
Friendship qualities

Ask the group the following question, and invite everyone to answer in turn:

If you could be best friends with anyone in the world, who would it be?

Then give each person a 'pack of words' and explain that these words represent desirable qualities in a friend.

Ask the young people (individually) to put the words in order, from most to least important, of qualities they look for in a friend.

Invite each young person to share what they've decided, and why.

Now, using the larger 'pack of words' ask the whole group to decide on an order together.

Scenarios
Friendship types

Place different friendship profiles (see pages 56–57) around the room.

Ask the group to read each one and decide whether they would choose to be that person's friend. If they would choose to befriend a person, they should write their name in the 'I would be your friend' space on the profile sheet.

Afterwards, find out whose profile was the most popular, and why. Encourage the group to reflect on how easy it is to choose friends based on first impressions. Ask them if they have done this in the past.

Remind the group that it is important to spend time getting to know someone before making a judgement about them.

Reflection
Healthy and unhealthy relationships

Give out sticky notes of two different colours, and pens. Invite the group to write down the parts of friendship that are healthy (on one colour of sticky notes) and unhealthy (on the other colour).

Reflect together on the differences.

Game
Friendship 'Jenga' tower

Put the sticky notes with the healthy parts of friendship (from the reflection activity) on the 'Jenga' blocks and build the 'Jenga' blocks into a tower.

As a group, play Jenga. Whilst playing, encourage the group to think about who they are friends with. Do any of them have any stories or experiences of positive or negative friendships? What did they do in the situation?

Be aware that, for some young people, this may be a particularly difficult area, so ensure you have appropriate support in place outside of this session – and remind the young people that this is available.

Discussion
Healthy relationships

Invite the young people to split into small groups of two or three. Give them a few minutes to discuss the following questions, then call them back together for a short time of feedback and sharing.

- *Why are healthy relationships important?*
- *How can you hold on to who you are in the face of peer pressure?*
- *Are relationships really worth all the hard work they sometimes require?*
- *What unique qualities do you bring to your friendships?*

Creative space
Friendship wristband reminders
(strands of thick cotton in various colours, beads or charms (optional))

Place strands of cotton (and beads or charms, if you have them) on a table in the middle of the group. Invite the young people to choose three strands each. Suggest that they each decide on the three most important qualities in a friendship and then choose one of their strands to represent that quality.

Invite the group to weave their three strands together in whatever way they wish (plaiting, knotting etc). If you have charms/beads, you could invite the young people to add them as they weave, with each charm or bead representing a particular friend.

Encourage the group to wear their wristbands as a reminder for them to be a good friend to others and to remind them to look for positive qualities in those they choose to surround themselves with.

(The creative space activity for this session can easily be amended to suit your context. You simply need to choose an activity that involves three or more different elements that are woven together in some way.)

Faith exploration
Being friends with God

During the 'Friendship wristband reminder' activity (or another activity of your choosing) you could use the following questions to open up conversations with young people individually, or in small groups.

- *Did you know that Jesus had a really good group of friends in the Bible? (You could describe what some of Jesus' disciples were like, and how Jesus was accountable with them.)*
- *Would you say you are friends with God?*
- *How do you think you can experience being God's friend?*

You could also ask a leader to share a personal testimony that explores their own relationship of friendship with God.

WHAT'S AROUND ME?

Objective:

- For young people to reflect on what influences their everyday life.

SOCIAL MEDIA AND INFLUENCES

This session will give your group space to explore how social media impacts their lives; as well as making space for each young person to consider their own sense of self-worth.

Suggested activities

Introduction
Revisit the previous session

Remind the young people of the theme from the last session and invite them to respond to the following questions:

Has anything happened since we last met that made you think about our last session together?

If so, what was it, and what did it make you think about?

Game
Chocolate choices
(a tub of small chocolates (eg Heroes, Celebrations etc))

Place a tub of small chocolates in the middle of your group and ask everyone to take one of each type of chocolate.

Then ask everyone to arrange the chocolates in order of their least favourite to most favourite.

Once everyone has shared their preferred chocolate order, note that everyone's opinions are different and then allow your group to eat their chocolates!

(If there is anyone in your group who cannot eat chocolate, make sure to have an alternative sweet treat available.)

Reflection
My everyday

Using drama, paper, storyboards, or even a list, ask each young person to reflect on their everyday life. Encourage them to think about the things they watch, people they speak to, social media they browse, food they eat. Notice the similarities and differences between the 'everydays' that are shared.

Creative space
Circles of influence

Ask each person in the group to draw a picture of themselves (it can be a stick figure) with three or four concentric circles around the outside.

Explain that each circle represents a different kind of

relationship – friends, family, teachers, youth workers, shopkeepers, YouTubers, bands, extended family etc. Invite the group to reflect on who has the most influence on their lives, and to label their circles appropriately – the relationships with the strongest influence should be closest to the centre.

Reflection
Avatar expectations

Invite the group to share their thoughts on social media. You might like to use the following questions to stimulate discussion:

- *How easy is it for someone to have a presence on social media that looks completely different to reality?*

- *How does social media influence your decisions, choices and mood?*

- *Do you think social media is a positive or negative influence?*

Ask the group if they know what an 'avatar' is in terms of social media. If they aren't sure, explain that an avatar is a 'digital representation' of a person that is used to represent someone online.

Hand out pens and paper and invite each young person to draw an avatar that represents what they feel they should be like.

For example, they might feel pressurised to have certain opinions, look a certain way, act in a certain way, etc.

Then ask each young person to create another avatar that represents who they really are.

Ask:

- *What differences do you see between your two avatars?*
- *Do you feel there is an expectation to look or be a certain way?*
- *Do you feel your social media presence is an honest reflection of who you are?*
- *How can we learn to celebrate who we are?*

If the group doesn't enjoy drawing, this activity can be done in other ways – eg junk modelling, computer design, magazine cut-outs or with sticky-note labels.

Conclude this activity by asking if anyone feels comfortable sharing their avatar(s). If a young person is brave enough to share, make sure that you reassure them that who they are is more than enough.

Faith exploration
God's influence

During the 'Avatar expectations' activity (or another activity of your choosing) you could use the following questions to open up conversations with young people individually, or in small groups.

- *What do you think God thinks of social media?*
- *What do you think Jesus' Instagram would look like?*
- *Have you ever chatted to God when you are feeling low about yourself?*
- *Did you know that God really cares about how you see yourself? He wants you to know that you are incredible!*

You could also ask a leader to share a personal testimony about finding their worth in what God says about them.

WHAT DO I VALUE?

Objective:

- To help young people reflect on how they can invest in their well-being – mentally, physically and spiritually.

HEALTHY EATING AND WHOLE BODY WELL-BEING

For many young people, issues around mental health and well-being can be a challenging area. But that doesn't mean it's something that should be avoided. Obviously, this session may highlight where extra help is needed for some young people – take some time beforehand to research where best to find suitable additional advice and support.

Suggested activities

Introduction
Revisit the previous session

Remind the young people of the theme from the last session and invite them to respond to the following questions:

Has anything happened since we last met that made you think about our last session together?

If so, what was it, and what did it make you think about?

Game
Pass the picture

Give each person a sheet of paper and ask them to draw a head and neck, then fold the paper over at the top and pass it to the next person, going round in a circle. They should ensure the bottom of the neck is still visible. The next person should draw a torso that joins onto the neck, and fold the paper again, leaving the bottom of the torso visible. The next person should draw the top half of a pair of legs, the next person the bottom of the legs, and then the final person, the feet.

The folded paper should be passed on one more time and then unfolded. The pictures should be shared with the rest of the group.

Game
Guess the value
(a selection of product/object images taken from various websites/magazines (you should make a note of the price of the products/objects), sticky notes, pens)

Spread out a selection of product/object images (with no price labels) for the group to see.

Give out sticky notes and pens and encourage the young people to guess the value of each product/object. They should write their guess on a sticky note and stick it on the image.

Reveal the price and see how close the young people were with their guesses.

Ask the group to think about their most valued possession and/or person. Discuss together why they are so valuable.

Provide each young person with a copy of the 'body parts' list (from page 58).

Ask them to work individually or in small groups to rank the different parts in order of their value.

You might like to use the following questions to get them thinking:

Which part of the human body could you live without?
Which part of the human body is vital?

Allow a few minutes for the group to decide on their ranking, and then invite them to share their decisions with others. Be prepared for some disagreement!

Then ask each young person to take a few minutes to look back through the list of body parts and consider which they invest the most time and value into with regard to their own bodies.

Video
Self-esteem

If you are working with a group who are particularly struggling with self-esteem, allow space for this to be explored further. There are several thought-provoking videos available online which may help to start a discussion, such as those created by 'Dove' in the United States.

Alternatively, there are suggestions for extending and further developing a conversation in this area at the back of this booklet.

(a large sheet/roll of paper, pens and pencils)

Ask a volunteer to lay on a large sheet of paper, and draw round them. Invite the group to think about the ways they can choose to invest in their own value, and write them on the body outline.

As a whole group, take some time to reflect on how we can look after our health and well-being.

(The group will naturally draw out specific areas that interest them, such as: habits for good mental health, body care or healthy eating/living, etc. If the group is particularly engaged in discussion and has lots of questions, you could develop this theme in future sessions.)

Reflection
Investing in me

It's very rare for a young person to be given the opportunity to reflect on how they can invest in themselves.

Encourage them to take a few minutes to think about their habits and behaviours, identifying anything they do that might not be having a positive impact on their life.

Areas to consider might include:

- *the people they hang out with*
- *the social media posts they read*
- *the videos they watch*
- *the food they eat*
- *the hobbies they have*

Ask the young people to consider whether or not these things help them to be the best version of themselves. Invite them to think about how they can challenge themselves to ensure that the choices they make are helping them both mentally, physically and spiritually.

Invite each young person to think of a positive investment they could make for their well-being. Depending on your group, you could do this through a graffiti-wall activity, writing a letter to yourself, writing a journal, kicking a ball into a net and saying what your positive investment will be.

Some examples might include:

- *I choose not to use my phone for an hour before bed*
- *I choose to eat five portions of fruit and vegetables every day*
- *I choose to spend time enjoying nature*
- *I choose to start running*
- *I choose to stay away from negative influences*

Faith exploration
Spiritual well-being

During the 'Investing in me' activity (or another activity of your choosing), you could share some key Bible verses that speak about self-care such as: 1 Corinthians 6:19,20; 1 Peter 3:4; Romans 12:2; Philippians 4:8; 3 John 1:2.

You might also like to use the following questions to open up conversations with the young people individually, or in small groups.

- *If you were mates with God, how would you involve him in your life?*
- *Does faith influence your life decisions?*
- *What could you do ito nvest in your own spiritual well-being?*
- *Did you know you can always talk with God about what's going on in your mind?*

You could also ask a leader to share a personal testimony about their well-being and faith.

Since issues around self-esteem, healthy eating and whole body well-being can be especially challenging for many young people, you might like to include a prayer request or question box in your meeting space. You could provide cards for young people to write on and leave in the box – giving them an opportunity to raise any specific concerns or needs.

CAN I BE BRAVE?

Objective:

- For young people to learn a new skill, and to gain confidence in their own abilities.

TRYING A NEW SKILL

For many young people the idea of doing something new and different is scary – what if they fail? It's easy to think that once we reach a certain age that starting something new is impossible – but this isn't true! Today's session will encourage your group to be bold and brave, to experiment and to understand the value in both failure and success.

Suggested activities

Introduction
Revisit the previous session

Remind the young people of the theme from the last session and invite them to respond to the following questions:

Has anything happened since we last met that made you think about our last session together?

If so, what was it, and what did it make you think about?

Creative space
Trying a new skill

This activity will form the main part of your session. You should choose an activity that suits your context, budget and skill set. If possible, you should try to choose an activity that will be new to all the young people in your group.

Examples include:

- *Trying a new sport*
- *Learning how to cook*
- *Creating a pin board*
- *Going jogging*
- *Learning how to draw or paint*
- *Learning wood carving*
- *Going to a dance workshop*
- *Learning to knit*
- *Learning a new game*

Whichever activity you choose, make sure that you have an intentional conversation with the young people as they participate. You might like to use the following questions:

- *If you could try something new, what would it be?*
- *Is there something you wish you had tried when you were younger?*
- *What prevents you from trying new things?*
- *Are you afraid of failure? Why?*
- *Have you experienced failure before?*
- *How can failure be a good thing?*
- *Have your past experiences made you reluctant to try new things?*
- *What would give you the confidence to try something new?*

At the end of your session, make time for the group to reflect on what they have accomplished.

Faith exploration
Taking risks with God

During the 'Trying a new skill' activity, alongside the questions listed above, you could use the following questions to open up conversations about faith with the young people individually, or in small groups.

- *Have you ever taken a risk?*
- *Would you say knowing Jesus is like an adventure or is it something boring?*
- *Have you ever chatted to God about the choices you make?*
- *Share about Peter choosing to follow Jesus and 'stepping out'.*

You could also ask a leader to share a personal testimony about what it is like learning to follow Jesus. It might be helpful for the person sharing their story to refer to a particular Bible passage, such as Peter stepping out of the boat to walk on the water towards Jesus, in Matthew 14.

Don't be afraid to ask the young people if they would like you to pray with them – for many, this will be another new thing to try!

WHAT DOES THE FUTURE HOLD?

Objective:

- For young people to build confidence and self-esteem through setting realistic goals.

DREAMS AND ASPIRATIONS

Everyone should have life goals and aspirations, big ones, small ones, and ones in between! Part of becoming an adult is recognising these goals and aspirations for the future and making plans that will help them to become reality.
In this session, your group will have the opportunity to explore how they can make small steps towards their goals, and discover the things that sometimes hold them back or get in the way of progress.

Suggested activities

Introduction
Revisit the previous session

Remind the young people of the theme from the last session and invite them to respond to the following questions:

Has anything happened since we last met that made you think about our last session together?

If so, what was it, and what did it make you think about?

Game
Smarties and straws
(Smarties (or similar sweets), drinking straws, 4 bowls)

Divide the group of young people into two teams and challenge them to compete in a relay race.

Place a bowl full of Smarties (or other similar sweets) in front of each team, and then put an empty bowl for each team at a distance. Each team member should be given a straw. Team members must take it in turns to make a Smartie stick to the bottom of their straw (by sucking – ensuring that the Smarties are too big to go up the straws!) and transport it over to the other bowl.

Set a time limit – and the winning team is the one with the most Smarties in the second bowl!

Discussion
Famous failures
(Images of easily recognised famous people (either printed or on screen))

Invite the group to look at the images of famous people and see if they recognise any of them.

Then ask the group the following questions:

- *Do you think any of these people are successful?*
- *Do you think any of them have ever failed in any way?*
- *How do you think they dealt with failure?*

Remind the group that failure is a key component to success – without failing we never learn how to do things differently.

Encourage the group to talk about times they have failed and tried again.

Then, in small groups, discuss the following questions:

- *Who inspires you?*
- *What are your goals in life?*
- *Why do you think people have different aspirations and goals?*

Reflection
Goal envelopes
(pens, paper, envelopes)

Split the young people into small groups and invite them to share their life-goals with one another.

Then invite them to individually write down their goals on a sheet of paper. They should follow each goal with at least three steps they need to take to make that goal a reality.

Once they have done this, they should place the sheet of paper with their goals on it in an envelope.

On the outside of the envelope they should then write or draw words or pictures that represent the kind of person they need to be in order to achieve their goals.

For example, if a young person's goal is 'to go to university', three steps towards that goal might be 'to work hard at school, to apply to the best university they can, to look into finance options available'. Then on the front of their envelope they might write that they need to be 'committed'.

Be aware that talking about the future can be a very sensitive subject, especially with the amount of pressure young people are faced with in school. Ensure that the session allows everyone in your group to explore future dreams in all areas of life.

Creative space
Self-portraits
(pens, pencils, art materials, paper)

Invite the group to draw self-portraits (emphasise that they don't need to be incredible works of art!). As they draw, encourage them to think about where they would like to be in five years.

If your group is not particularly 'arty', you might like to use a different activity that will enable the young people to reflect on the same theme.

Faith exploration
God has big dreams for you

During the 'Self-portraits' activity (or another activity of your choosing), you could share a story from the Bible about someone who persevered in the face of something that seemed impossible, such as:

- *David when he fought Goliath (1 Samuel 17)*
- *Daniel in the lion's den (Daniel 6)*
- *Moses and the Red Sea (Exodus 14).*

You might also choose to use the following questions to open up conversations with the young people individually, or in small groups.

- *Do you think you have free will?*
- *Have you ever thought about God having a plan for your life?*
- *Did you know that God has big dreams for you?*
- *Have you ever shared your dreams with God?*

You could also ask a leader to share a personal testimony about their own life-goals, and how these connect to their faith. If appropriate, they might also like to include a part of their story that shows how they worked through failure, leading to success.

ALL WRAPPED UP?

Objective:

- To draw this particular set of sessions to a close and plan together for the future.

WHAT NEXT?

This session gives time for the group to reflect on what they have discovered about themselves over the past nine weeks. It will also give them the opportunity to share which topics/ themes they would like to continue exploring.

Suggested activities

Introduction
Recap of themes

Display the themes from each of the previous sessions around the room and ask the group to think back over what each of the sessions covered.

Invite the group to share their thoughts, comments and reactions as they remember what has been discussed.

Reflection
String evaluation
(a ball of wool)

Pass a ball of wool around the group, inviting each individual (when they are holding the wool) to say something they have learned, been challenged about, or enjoyed. After each person shares, they pass the wool on to someone else, unravelling it as they go, and keeping hold of their part of the string.

Once everyone has contributed, pass the ball of wool back (in reverse order to avoid tangles!) around the group. This time, invite each individual to share an idea for how they would like the group to go forward. After each person shares, they pass the wool on to the next person and wind up the ball of wool as they go.

Reflection
Evaluation forms

Hand out evaluation forms for the group to complete (see page 59).

Activity
Celebration

Conclude your time together with a fun celebration. Depending on your context, you could make this into a social event at another venue, eg going bowling or you could share in a simple activity together, like biscuit decorating.

Faith exploration
What about God?

During your celebration activity, you could use the following questions to open up conversations with the young people individually, or in small groups.

- *Do you think differently about God compared to when we first started our Rooted group?*

- *If you could ask God anything, what would it be?*

What's next?

Hopefully, your group will have enjoyed spending time together and having the opportunity to think about faith and life. Maintaining the relationships that have been formed is vital, not only for faith development, but for growing an authentic community that is a safe space for young people.

Remember, this is not the end, it's only the beginning!

A few ideas for going forward as a group:

- *Set up a discipleship group to explore the Bible together.*

- *Establish a drop-in lunch club in a local school that explores questions that your group has asked.*

- *Invite members of your Rooted group to join a local youth group.*

- *Establish a mentoring programme, through which each young person can benefit from additional support.*

EXTRA IDEAS

The themes in this resource pack are broad and varied, and have the potential to be explored in a multitude of ways.

Aside from the session details already outlined, you could use some of the following ideas as you unpack each theme. You might also choose to extend your Rooted programme by further developing each of these ideas into a whole session for your group.

WHAT IS MY NAME?
Exploring identity

Sharing interests
You could invite each individual in your group to share one of their interests/hobbies each week. This could be a brief 5-minute feature in your session, or you might choose to build an entire session around each interest – encouraging the group to share their skills and experiences with one another.

Identity on canvas
You could dedicate an extended period of time or even a whole session to the 'Creative space' activity outlined on page 9. Each young person could create a large canvas that represents their identity.

Blogs and journals

You could invite each young person in your group to start a blog or a journal that they could add to after each Rooted session. Their blog or journal could be a space to explore questions like:

- *What do I like about myself?*

- *Who am I?*

- *What kind of person do I want to be and why?*

- *What did I hear during the Rooted session today that made me think?*

- *What questions do I have after my time at the Rooted session today?*

WHAT'S MY JOURNEY?
Sharing stories

My family story

You could invite the young people in your group to explore their family history (obviously this could be a sensitive topic for some – so decide carefully if this is appropriate for your group). They could do this before, during or after a session and share what they have learned with the rest of the group.

My local story

You could take some time to explore the story of your local area/town/city with your group (making sure you have appropriate parental permissions in place).

You could invite each young person to make a short film about their own daily life, entitled 'A day in the life of...'. These could then be shared as part of your session, or depending on the size of your group and the length of the films created, this might form a whole 'sharing stories' session.

WHAT DO I FEEL?
Understanding emotions

Particular emotions
You could spend a number of sessions exploring particular emotions. For example, you might choose to build a session around any of the following:
Anger, Happiness, Sadness, Fear, Disgust, etc

Inside Out
You might choose to watch the film *Inside Out* with your group (ensuring you have appropriate licensing permissions) – and use this as a tool to open up conversations around the emotions portrayed in the film.

Experiencing emotion
Depending on your group, using a tool such as drama, dance or sport may help to facilitate conversations around emotions. For example, most sporting activities involve experiencing failure, working hard, working as a team etc. Each of these experiences can create a different emotional response.

HOW DO I SEE MYSELF?
Exploring self-worth

Talent show
You could invite the young people in your group to put on a talent show, either for themselves, or perhaps for your local community. This may be a helpful prompt for discussion around the gifts and skills of each young person in your group.

Community competition
You could host a sport competition for your community, inviting the young people either to talk part directly, or to be responsible for organising the event. Again, this may be a helpful prompt for discussion around the gifts and skills of each young person in your group.

WHO'S AROUND ME?
Friendship and choices

Exploring trust
Trust can be a complex issue for many young people – and spending some extra time exploring this with your group may be beneficial. You could dedicate a whole session to this, exploring how trust can be broken and how trust can be built.

(Exploring this topic may raise some significant pastoral issues for members of your group – so before you do this, ensure you have an appropriate system of support in place,

including knowledge of appropriate routes for referral for any additional help that may be required.)

Sex and relationships

Depending on your group, you could take several sessions to explore issues around sex and relationships. You might choose to cover questions, such as:

- *What makes a healthy relationship?*
- *What makes an unhealthy relationship?*
- *What does sex mean, and when is sex appropriate?*
- *How can 'boundaries' be helpful in a relationship?*
- *What does it look like to look after yourself when you are in a relationship?*

Faith community

You could take the opportunity within this theme to explore the difference being part of a faith community can make to the challenges and adventures of life. You might choose to invite some members of your local Christian community to share their stories with your group – or you could simply invite the leaders of your group to share an extended version of their own faith stories.

WHAT'S AROUND ME?
Social media and influences

Social media

If the majority of your group are active on social media (which they probably are!), you could take a session or a number of sessions to explore various social media platforms.

Issues to focus on might include:

- *Internet safety*
- *Authenticity*
- *The influence of social media*
- *The strengths and weaknesses of different social media platforms*

Celebrity influence

Many young people are influenced by celebrity lifestyle. You could invite each young person to bring in a picture of their favourite celebrity – and invite them to share the influence this person has over their lives.

What I wear...

Knowing what is fashionable and what is not (in terms of clothing), and choosing your clothing accordingly can be a significant point of pressure for many young people.

You could arrange a visit to a local shopping centre (with appropriate parental permission) inviting your group to reflect on the clothing they see, the impression it makes and how it makes them feel.

Fashion show

You could host a fashion show in your community, inviting the young people to make outfits out of recycled materials. Either before or after the show, you could spend some time discussing the effects of clothing on self-esteem, but also where the influences come from that affect fashion choices.

What I watch...

Most young people watch an enormous amount of video content – via TV, streaming services, YouTube etc. You could invite each young person in the group to share a clip from their favourite programme/channel/series and discuss the following questions as a whole group:

- *How do you decide what to watch, and what not to watch?*
- *Do you think age ratings are helpful?*
- *Are you happy with the amount of time you spend watching video content?*
- *How much does what you watch influence your life?*

What I achieve...

The pressure to 'achieve' academically can be overwhelming for many young people. Depending on their school context and year group, some may feel this pressure more acutely than others. You could invite each young person in the group to share a little of their own experiences at school with regard to the pressure to 'achieve', and then discuss the following questions as a group:

- *How much pressure is too much pressure?*
- *How can you cope with the pressure of exams?*
- *Where can you go for extra help when you feel too pressured by school?*
- *Are you defined by your school grades – or is there more to who you are and who you will be?*

If your group is meeting during exam season, you could give space for discussion around this issue every time you meet. You might also consider inviting several leaders to share their own 'school achievement' story – especially those who have perhaps 'deviated' somewhat from the 'usual' route.

Come 'eat healthy' with me!

You could invite your group to participate in a session, or series of sessions, around healthy eating by hosting a 'Come dine with me' style event, in which each young person (or perhaps a small group of young people) is responsible for providing part of a healthy meal for the group. (Ensure you are aware of any allergies and dietary requirements).

Healthy food?

You could take your group to visit a local supermarket or community farm and talk about where their food comes from. As part of these conversations you could discuss what 'healthy eating' means for your group, and perhaps share some ideas for healthy recipes that would be easy for the members of your group to create at home.

Exercise matters

If appropriate for your group, you could focus each of your Rooted sessions around some form of physical exercise. Perhaps the same type of exercise each week, or perhaps something different every time you meet, such as:

- *Dance lessons*
- *Football*
- *Trampolining*
- *Swimming*

- *Following a fitness video*
- *Tennis*
- *Bike riding*

If you decide to include physical exercise as part of your session, make sure you have appropriate parental permission, along with following the risk assessment and health and safety procedures for your organisation.

Beautiful?

If appropriate for your group, you could visit a local beauty salon together as you talk about issues of self-esteem, self-image and self-care. Questions for discussion might include:

- *What is true beauty?*
- *Who decides what is beautiful and what is not?*
- *Why is it important to care for our own bodies?*
- *What does self-care look like for you?*

CAN I BE BRAVE?
Trying a new skill

Being brave

As described on page 37, the idea of doing something new can be scary for many young people. But, stepping out and being brave, within a supportive group environment, can be helpful for personal development and self-belief.

Extra ideas for new skills to explore include:

- *Rock climbing*
- *Abseiling*
- *Embroidery*
- *Zumba classes*
- *DJ lessons*
- *Graffiti lessons*
- *Archery*
- *Willow weaving*
- *Lessons in a foreign language*

If appropriate, you might choose to ask your group to come up with a project they all feel is impossible to achieve – you could then take steps to achieve this together!

WHAT DOES THE FUTURE HOLD?
Dreams and aspirations

The story so far
If you can, try finding a local person, who your group will relate to, and who is willing to share their 'success story' with the group. Ideally, this person should be able to share some 'life lessons' they've learned along the way and share what dreams and aspirations they still have for the future.

What will I do?
Find out what the young people in your group are interested in – what kind of work might they want to be involved with in the future? Depending on their interests, invite an

appropriate specialist to come and share their story, and perhaps share some of their skills with the group. People to invite might include:

- *Fire station staff*
- *Police officers*
- *Chefs*
- *Artists*
- *Actors*
- *Hairdressers*
- *Teachers (although not from a school any of the young people attend!)*

Understanding my potential

Many young people aren't sure how they see their future unfolding. Some find it a challenge to understand how their skills, gifts and personality could flourish.

You could use something like Myers-Briggs (led by an approved practitioner), or other personality profiling tests, to help your group explore their identity, and understand the strengths of their personalities and abilities.

Name: Josh

Age: 14

Favourite colour:
Black

Favourite school subject:
Music

Favourite type of music:
Acoustic

Strengths:
patient, good listener, good cook

Other details:
only child

I WOULD BE YOUR FRIEND:

Name: Kymba

Age: 11

Favourite colour:
Purple

Favourite school subject:
Textiles

Favourite type of music:
Pop

Strengths:
good fashion sense, loyal, honest

Other details:
wheelchair user

I WOULD BE YOUR FRIEND:

Name: Jo

Age: 13

Favourite colour:
Green

Favourite school subject:
Maths

Favourite type of music:
Doesn't like music

Strengths:
friendly, good sense of humour, fun

Other details:
asylum seeker, doesn't speak much English

I WOULD BE YOUR FRIEND:

Name: Ellie

Age: 12

Favourite colour:
Blue

Favourite school subject:
Hates school!

Favourite type of music:
Boy bands

Strengths:
chatty, amazing artist, really creative

Other details:
low self-esteem

I WOULD BE YOUR FRIEND:

Name: Jordan

Age: 16

Favourite colour:
Black

Favourite school subject:
Religious Education

Favourite type of music:
Rock

Strengths:
works hard, stands up against peer pressure, honest

Other details:
goes to church and sings in a choir

I WOULD BE YOUR FRIEND:

Name: Sula

Age: 15

Favourite colour:
Orange

Favourite school subject:
P.E.

Favourite type of music:
Reggae

Strengths:
good song-writer, friendly, polite

Other details:
smokes dope

I WOULD BE YOUR FRIEND:

Name: Naomi

Age: 13

Favourite colour:
Grey

Favourite school subject:
Art

Favourite type of music:
Hip-hop

Strengths:
has lots of friends, outgoing, adventurous

Other details:
attention seeking personality

I WOULD BE YOUR FRIEND:

Name: Samantha

Age: 13

Favourite colour:
Pale pink

Favourite school subject:
Chemistry

Favourite type of music:
Dance

Strengths:
brave, bold, confident

Other details:
in foster care, and is a diabetic

I WOULD BE YOUR FRIEND:

WHAT'S THE MOST IMPORTANT?

Rank the following parts of body in order of their importance. 1 = the most important, 25 = the least important.

toenails ☐
ears ☐
brain ☐
heart ☐
eyes ☐
lungs ☐
stomach ☐
intestines ☐
gall bladder ☐
fingers ☐
legs ☐
teeth ☐
nose ☐
belly button ☐
elbows ☐
armpits ☐
spinal cord ☐
blood ☐
arms ☐
liver ☐
kidneys ☐
skin ☐
toes ☐
knees ☐
tongue ☐

WHAT'S THE MOST IMPORTANT?

Rank the following parts of body in order of their importance. 1 = the most important, 25 = the least important.

toenails ☐
ears ☐
brain ☐
heart ☐
eyes ☐
lungs ☐
stomach ☐
intestines ☐
gall bladder ☐
fingers ☐
legs ☐
teeth ☐
nose ☐
belly button ☐
elbows ☐
armpits ☐
spinal cord ☐
blood ☐
arms ☐
liver ☐
kidneys ☐
skin ☐
toes ☐
knees ☐
tongue ☐

WHAT'S THE MOST IMPORTANT?

Rank the following parts of body in order of their importance. 1 = the most important, 25 = the least important.

toenails ☐
ears ☐
brain ☐
heart ☐
eyes ☐
lungs ☐
stomach ☐
intestines ☐
gall bladder ☐
fingers ☐
legs ☐
teeth ☐
nose ☐
belly button ☐
elbows ☐
armpits ☐
spinal cord ☐
blood ☐
arms ☐
liver ☐
kidneys ☐
skin ☐
toes ☐
knees ☐
tongue ☐

Rooted ALL ABOUT ME

Name:

_____

Age:

_____

Favourite chocolate bar:

_____

My name means:

_____

If I had to describe myself in one word it would be:

My favourite thing about me is:

_____

_____

If I were a flavour of ice cream, I would be...

_____

There is no right or wrong answer, no box that is better than another. Don't forget we are all unique and this is about YOU!

Tick the box that best describes how you feel about each of the following statements:

I am confident in who I am

All the time	Most of the time	Sometimes	Never
◯	◯	◯	◯

I am brave

All the time	Most of the time	Sometimes	Never
◯	◯	◯	◯

I know how to describe what I am feeling

All the time	Most of the time	Sometimes	Never
◯	◯	◯	◯

I like myself

All the time	Most of the time	Sometimes	Never
◯	◯	◯	◯

I know what I want to do with my life

All the time	Most of the time	Sometimes	Never
◯	◯	◯	◯

I make healthy choices

All the time	Most of the time	Sometimes	Never
◯	◯	◯	◯

Rooted MY JOURNEY

How would you rate your experience of Rooted?

○ Excellent - loved every minute!

○ Good - I enjoyed most of it

○ Alright - I could take it or leave it

○ Rubbish - Never again!

Which session did you enjoy the most and why?

_____

_____

What one thing would you change and why?

_____

_____

Would you recommend Rooted to a friend?

Yes ○   No ○

Why?

_____

_____

There is no right or wrong answer, no box that is better than another. Don't forget we are all unique and this is about YOU!

Tick the box that best describes how you feel about each of the following statements:

I am confident in who I am

All the time   Most of the time   Sometimes   Never
○   ○   ○   ○

I am brave

All the time   Most of the time   Sometimes   Never
○   ○   ○   ○

I know how to describe what I am feeling

All the time   Most of the time   Sometimes   Never
○   ○   ○   ○

I like myself

All the time   Most of the time   Sometimes   Never
○   ○   ○   ○

I know what I want to do with my life

All the time   Most of the time   Sometimes   Never
○   ○   ○   ○

I make healthy choices

All the time   Most of the time   Sometimes   Never
○   ○   ○   ○

BUT HOW DO I CONNECT WITH A GROUP OF YOUNG PEOPLE IN THE FIRST PLACE?

Unless you're already working with an established group of young people, you might be wondering how you can begin to make initial connections with young people in your community.

Developing a Rooted Hub

To help you make initial connections, we recommend that you create a Rooted Hub in your community. A Rooted Hub is a safe space for young people to gather - similar to the kinds of spaces used for 'drop-in' youthwork.

A Rooted Hub should:

- *provide a safe, welcoming, accessible environment for young people to gather*

- *provide activities for young people to engage in which are appropriate for their context*

- *use contemporary media and interests to facilitate honest and authentic conversations*

- *offer young people a chance to 'go deeper' by joining a 'Rooted' group*

What kind of space should be used for a Rooted Hub?

Any space - indoor or outdoor that can be made safe, welcoming and accessible for young people!

Ideally your location should be somewhere that young people in your community are already familiar with, feel comfortable coming to and are able to travel to easily.

Consider what facilities you will need based on what kind of activities you want to offer.

What kind of activities should a Rooted Hub provide?
A Rooted Hub should be based around activities that connect with the young people in your community. For example, if there are a group of young people who are interested in songwriting, your hub should provide activities around this theme.

Whatever your theme, you should try to find at least one volunteer who is skilled in that particular area and is able to share their talents with the young people.

Ideas for hub themes could include:

- *Board games*
- *Songwriting*
- *Film or TV*
- *Photography*
- *A particular sport*
- *Street art*
- *Music*
- *Food*

How do Rooted Hub activities help to facilitate honest and authentic conversations?
Meeting young people where they are and journeying alongside them is one of the core principles of Rooted.

Engaging with young people through activities that they are already interested in and care about leads to authentic and meaningful conversations.

The key is to invite young people to share their interests with you, asking insightful, thoughtful and open questions, and taking the time to listen to what they say.

If your Rooted Hub is based around music, and you decide to ask the young people to share some of their favourite songs with you, questions may include:

- *Why do you like this song?*
- *What does it mean to you?*
- *How does listening to this song make you feel?*
- *What kind of person does this song make you want to be?*
- *Why do you like this artist? Do you like any more of their songs?*
- *When do you most often listen to this music?*

Obviously, you will need to carefully consider which questions to ask, based on your hub theme and context.

If you'd like a few pointers for how to open up this kind of conversation, you can buy a set of Rooted Hub conversation cards (which work with any theme) from the Scripture Union website.

A note on safeguarding and insurance...
All Rooted Hubs must abide by the safeguarding policy of your organisation.

Depending on your activities and location, you may need specific insurance cover (outside of that which your organisation normally provides). Consult with your insurance provider for more information.